MW01610996

by Farra Allen

 HOUGHTON MIFFLIN HARCOURT
School Publishers

PHOTOGRAPHY CREDITS: Cover © Peter Adams Photography/Alamy; 1 © MedioImages/Corbis; 2 © Mary-Ella Keith/Alamy; 3 © Medio Images/Corbis; 4 © Image100/Corbis; 5 © Reimar Gaertner/Alamy; 6 © Peter Adams Photography/Alamy; 7 © Jonathan Plant/Alamy; 8 © Thinkstock/Corbis; 9 © Greg Vaughn/Alamy; 10 © Jose Azel/Getty Images/Aurora Creative

Printed in China

ISBN-13: 978-0-547-02753-1
ISBN-10: 0-547-02753-2

3 4 5 6 7 8 0940 18 17 16 15 14 13 12 11 10

sun

tree

Look at the sun.
It is in the sky.
The sun can help
the trees grow.

birds

Look at the birds.
They like to sit
in the trees.

grass

Look at the sun.
It is in the sky.
It can help
the grass grow.

COWS

Look at the cows.
The cows like to eat
the grass.

plants

Look at the sun.
It is in the sky.
It can help
the plants grow.

rabbit

Look at the rabbit.
It likes to eat
the plants.

apples

Look at the sun.
It is in the sky.
The sun can help
the apples grow.

Look at us.
We like to pick
the apples.

And we can eat
the apples!

Responding

✔ TARGET SKILL **Main Ideas and Details** What is the main idea of this story? What are the details? Make a word web.

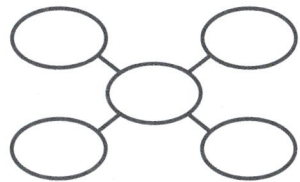

✏️ **Talk About It**

Text to World What can people do when the sun is out?

around	carry
because	light
before	show
bring	think

TARGET SKILL **Main Ideas and Details** Tell important ideas and details about a topic.

TARGET STRATEGY **Question** Ask questions about what you are reading.

GENRE Informational text gives facts about a topic.